SPEAK UP!
CONFRONTING DISCRIMINATION IN YOUR DAILY LIFE™

CONFRONTING
LGBTQ+
DISCRIMINATION

AVERY ELIZABETH HURT

Rosen YA

New York

Published in 2018 by The Rosen Publishing Group, Inc.
29 East 21st Street, New York, NY 10010

Library of Congress Cataloging-in-Publication Data

Names: Hurt, Avery Elizabeth, author.
Title: Confronting LGBTQ+ discrimination / Avery Elizabeth Hurt.
Description: New York: Rosen Publishing, 2018. | Series: Speak up! Confronting discrimination in your daily life | Includes bibliographical references and index. | Audience: Grades 7–12.
Identifiers: LCCN 2017017641| ISBN 9781538381748 (library bound) | ISBN 9781538381724 (pbk.) | ISBN 9781538381731 (6 pack)
Subjects: LCSH: Homophobia—United States—Juvenile literature. | Sexual minorities—Civil rights—United States—Juvenile literature. | Discrimination—United States—Juvenile literature.
Classification: LCC HQ76.45.U5 H87 2018 | DDC 306.76—dc23
LC record available at https://lccn.loc.gov/2017017641

Manufactured in China

33614080877995

CONTENTS

INTRODUCTION   4

CHAPTER ONE
THE GOOD, THE BAD, AND THE ILLEGAL   8

CHAPTER TWO
IT'S NOT JUST THEM   16

CHAPTER THREE
DISCRIMINATION HAPPENS   24

CHAPTER FOUR
CHANGING YOUR SCHOOL   31

CHAPTER FIVE
CHANGING THE WORLD   39

CHAPTER SIX
THE FUTURE   47

GLOSSARY   54
FOR MORE INFORMATION   56
FOR FURTHER READING   58
BIBLIOGRAPHY   59
INDEX   62

INTRODUCTION

Times have certainly changed. Prior to 1973, the American Psychological Association (APA) listed homosexuality as a mental disorder. In 2015, the Supreme Court ruled that same-sex couples have a constitutional right to marry. In the interim forty-two years, a substantial body of scientific research (and a great deal of common sense) finally persuaded the APA that being LGBTQ+ was not in fact a mental disorder. After the Supreme Court ruled it was unacceptable to deny same-sex couples the marriage rights afforded to other couples, many Americans' attitudes toward LGBTQ+ people changed rapidly.

According to Gallup's 2016 Mood of the Nation survey, 60 percent of Americans are satisfied with the level of acceptance of gays and lesbians in the United States. That's up from 53 percent in 2015, and only 32 percent as recently as 2006. And when the survey lens is fixed on people age eighteen to thirty, that percentage jumps to 80–92. So, that's the good news. But for people who identify as lesbian, gay, bisexual, transgender, queer, or who are sexually or gender nonconforming in other ways (LGBTQ+), discrimination is still a fact of everyday life.

The Federal Civil Rights laws that protect Americans' rights based on race and gender do not cover sexual orientation. A gay couple can legally marry in all fifty states, but could in many states lose their jobs for

People all over the United States—and the world—celebrated the Supreme Court ruling that made gay marriage legal throughout the fifty states.

exercising that right. Not only may LGBTQ+ people (married or not) be fired, they can also be evicted from their homes, denied service at restaurants, denied credit, and excluded from juries. It can be difficult for them to adopt children, buy health or life insurance, or get into college. And in many states, all of this is still perfectly legal.

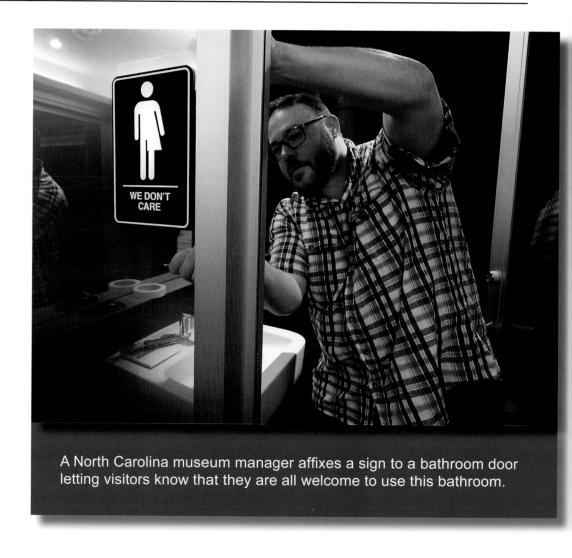

A North Carolina museum manager affixes a sign to a bathroom door letting visitors know that they are all welcome to use this bathroom.

In fact, many people who identify as LGBTQ+ don't have to wait until they're adults to learn what discrimination is like. LGBTQ+ students can be excluded from clubs and school organizations and face resistance when they try to form their own clubs. They have been mocked and bullied by fellow students and sometimes by teachers as well. Transgender students face additional problems regarding restroom and locker room access, and many LGBTQ+ students feel isolated and even unsafe at school.

Students have difficulty finding information about LGBTQ+ sexuality and other issues. In several states, laws prevent teachers from discussing homosexuality in class. In one case, when a seventeen-year-old gay student in Utah asked his health teacher about safe sex, he was told that the teacher was not allowed to talk about it. Though some schools have enacted anti-discrimination policies that protect LGBTQ+ students, many more have not. And often the policies that do exist are ignored or poorly enforced.

Despite all of this, progress is still being made. It sometimes seems that when it comes to LGBTQ+ discrimination, the United States takes a step back for every two steps forward. But those forward steps are huge ones, and if everyone just keeps marching, LGBTQ+ discrimination will one day be a thing of the past.

CHAPTER ONE

THE GOOD, THE BAD, AND THE ILLEGAL

Discrimination is not always bad. One definition of the word is simply "the quality or power of finely distinguishing." An avid gamer would likely discriminate between various video game consoles. People are using their powers of discrimination whenever they say something like "I prefer science fiction to thrillers," or "I like math, but chemistry, not so much." There is nothing bad about that, though it might not be great for their chemistry grades!

One can even discriminate between people in perfectly harmless ways. You may prefer to spend time with your soccer mates on the weekend rather than your friends from school—and that's okay. Discrimination becomes a problem when it is used to exclude certain people from places and activities that are open to all others, or to treat people differently based on categories such as the color of their skin, their ancestors' place of origin, whom and how they worship, whom they love, or what gender they are. When one group of people chooses to deny another their rights, they are engaging in bad discrimination.

Discriminating between objects or activities is not the same as discriminating among people—though it's still a good idea to make wise choices.

WHAT DISCRIMINATION LOOKS LIKE

You can find discrimination almost everywhere. When women or people of color are paid less than white men for doing the same job or when minorities are passed over in favor of nonminority job applicants, this is discrimination in the workplace. Discrimination in housing occurs when a landlord refuses to rent to black, Jewish, or LGBTQ+ families. Discrimination in education

DEFINING THE TERMS

The phrase LGBTQ+ refers to a collection of sexual orientations and gender identities. Here is a breakdown of what those letters mean:

- **Lesbian:** A woman who is sexually attracted to other women.
- **Gay:** A person who is sexually attracted to people of their own gender. This term can be used by men or women, but often refers to men attracted to other men, while *lesbian* is used only for women.
- **Bisexual:** A person who is sexually attracted to both men and women.
- **Transgender:** A person who does not identify with the gender they were assigned at birth.
- **Queer:** A person whose sexual orientation or gender identity falls outside the heterosexual mainstream or the gender binary. This is often a kind of catch-all term, meaning one person may identify as both queer and lesbian whereas another may use the term "queer" because he or she falls along the gender spectrum but does not identify as male or female.
- Similar to the term "queer," the "plus" is always added for inclusivity's sake, to make sure any individual whose sexual orientation or gender identity is not covered by the acronym "LGBTQ" is still embraced. This often includes "I" (intersex), "A" (asexual), and nonbinary individuals, among others. And this list is always growing!

happens when college applicants are turned down for belonging to a minority, when a teacher calls on only the boys in a class (or only the girls), or when clubs or sports teams won't allow LGBTQ+ students to join. Racial slurs, insults, bullying, and hate speech aimed at minorities or marginalized groups are all forms of discrimination as well.

These kinds of discrimination are obvious, but discrimination can be subtle, too, and sometimes unintentional. Ignoring a female colleague when she contributes an idea at a meeting, encouraging African American students to try out for basketball but not to apply for scholarships, using the word "gay" to mean "bad"—all of these are quiet forms of discrimination called microaggressions. Sometimes the people who do these things do not mean any harm; they may even be completely unaware that they've discriminated against someone. Someone who says, "Oh, that's so gay!" may not realize they are spreading a subconscious message that being LGBTQ+ is uncool.

The problem with subtle discrimination is that it can be hard to prevent. When an action is not obviously a violation of someone's rights or is not technically illegal, it may be very difficult to right that wrong. When much of the discrimination being perpetrated against a group of people is subtle, both policy makers and the public may underestimate its extent in society—causing them to fail to support the laws necessary to prevent it.

This is, in part, what happened when in 2012 the Supreme Court invalidated key parts of the Voting Rights Act, which protected the rights of African Americans to vote. As a voice of the majority opinion in that case, Chief Justice John Roberts argued that racial discrimination in voting was no longer a serious enough issue to require the full protections offered by the 1965 law. He wrote, "Our country has changed, and while any racial discrimination in voting is too much, Congress must ensure that the legislation it passes to remedy that problem speaks to current conditions." African Americans who are still having trouble exercising their right to vote are painfully aware that voting discrimination has not ended—it has simply become more subtle, as overtly discriminatory poll taxes and literacy tests have given way to irregular hours at the registration office and far fewer polling places in poor communities.

A NEW NIGHT AT THE STONEWALL INN

On Friday evening, June 27, 1969, the popular gay bar Stonewall Inn in Greenwich Village, New York, was filled with regulars. In New York at this time—as in most US cities—public homosexuality was illegal. People who were LGBTQ+ met and socialized in private establishments and gay bars around the city. Police regularly raided these places and arrested and harassed the customers, who for the most part did not resist. But this time something was different. When the police arrived, a few people fought back. They threw things at the police, shouting "gay power" and refusing to get into the police wagons. Soon, a riot broke out. Eventually the police

ar 1969 07-02-69. Disturbance on Sheridan Square, NYC. Scenes at Christopher St. and 7th Ave. South with police trying to clear crowds. Pictured, Stonewall Inn which was raided one day last week.(Larry Morris/The New

The Stonewall Inn in 1969. When patrons stood up to police one night in 1969, they inspired similar protests all around the nation—and set off the nonviolent gay rights movement.

dispersed the crowd, but the next night more than 1,000 people arrived to continue rioting. Over the next few days, demonstrations against police harassment took place all around the city.

The Stonewall riots inspired LGBTQ+ people and their supporters in other towns and cities to stand up for LGBTQ+ rights, beginning what came to be known as the gay rights movement. Fortunately, most of the demonstrations inspired by the Stonewall riots were peaceful.

LGBTQ+ DISCRIMINATION

LGBTQ+ people in America began to publicly and loudly insist on their rights at about the same time as African Americans began to demand theirs in the 1960s. The Stonewall riots in New York City in 1969 are considered the true beginning of the Pride movement and the

LGBT workplace discrimination, state-by-state

Below are states with employment laws and policies that prohibit discrimination in the workplace based on sexual orientation and gender identity.

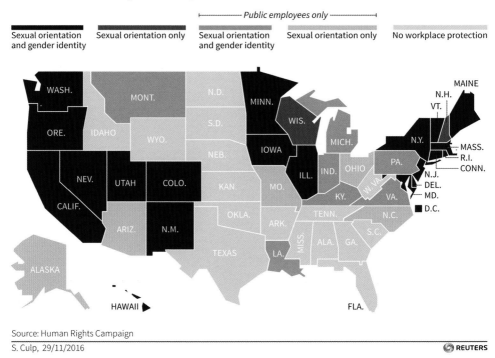

Source: Human Rights Campaign
S. Culp, 29/11/2016   REUTERS

The United States still has a lot of work ahead of it before the map becomes totally purple.

organized and concentrated effort to prevent LGBTQ+ discrimination. The fight for LGBTQ+ rights has met with a lot of success. The recent nationwide legalization of same-sex marriage was a huge win, but guaranteeing the right of same-sex couples to marry does not immediately guarantee LGBTQ+ citizens all the rights taken for granted by so many other people.

Today, roughly half a century after Stonewall, LGBTQ+ people still face a great deal of discrimination—being paid less for the same work, passed over for jobs or promotions, kicked out of apartments or turned down for mortgages, called insulting names, and alarmingly often, becoming victims of violence—simply because they are LGBTQ+. Transgender people face all of these problems and are also denied the use of public bathrooms and locker rooms, making it difficult for them to even enjoy public spaces or engage in routine business. The legalization of gay marriage, wonderful though it is, does not mean that the "current conditions" for the LGBTQ+ community are just fine and dandy.

Despite these problems and setbacks, the good news is overtaking the bad. Recall that a majority of Americans support LGBTQ+ rights, and those under the age of thirty do so overwhelmingly. We can expect future successes in the fight against LGBTQ+ discrimination. Unfortunately, the people in charge of making laws are not always so overwhelmingly supportive. It is still going to take some work to get the message out. Protecting LGBTQ+ people from discrimination will involve not only a working knowledge of civil rights laws and how to change them, but also a deep understanding of why people discriminate against other people.

CHAPTER TWO

IT'S NOT JUST THEM

t's easy to write off discrimination and the people who use it as mean and hateful. But simply condemning the actions or beliefs of another person does nothing to change them; it just makes you angry and puts the other person on the defensive. Discrimination can be a little easier to confront when you know where it comes from.

STONE AGE SKILLS

Classifying things into groups is not only natural to humans, it may even be necessary in some ways. The ability to sort things into categories, such as edible or not edible, animal who might eat me or animal who won't eat me, good camping spot or bad camping spot, had a lot to do with how our prehistoric ancestors survived to pass their genes along to us. When it came to social organization, being able to sort people into groups was probably pretty helpful to our ancient ancestors, too. Those guys with the rocks and clubs coming over the ridge may be a hunting party that left the group this morning, or they may be a tribe from the

The human tendency to distrust or dislike people who are different from us may go back a long way—hundreds of thousands of years back!

other side of the ridge coming to kill your tribe and take over your hunting grounds. Being able to quickly tell who's in your group and who's not was a handy skill—a few hundred thousand years ago. But in the modern

HOW TO TALK TO A BIGOT

In addition to fighting for the basic rights other people take for granted, many LGBTQ+ people have to deal with insults, slurs, and rude comments. Their straight friends and allies can help a lot by speaking up when they witness these things.

It doesn't take a sermon to make a point. When a person says something offensive—say, uses a derogatory slur or makes an anti-LGBTQ+ comment—you can calmly and politely say something like, "Those comments make me very uncomfortable. I believe LGBTQ+ people should be treated with the same respect as anyone else." It's usually more effective to state these objections from your point of view, saying, "It bothers me" or "I believe," rather than criticizing the speaker by saying things like, "It's so unkind to speak that way" or "You're such a bigot." Even if the speaker is an unkind bigot, you won't accomplish much by pointing that out, and you might just close off any chance of engaging in a constructive dialogue.

When that doesn't work, sometimes the best thing you can do is to be a role model. Show—rather than tell—others what nondiscrimination looks like.

world, just because someone belongs to a different group doesn't mean they pose an immediate threat.

Modern humans still have a tendency to distrust—and sometimes even reject or attack—people from other groups. Experts call this "tribal psychology," and even the most open, accepting people in the world probably still have a bit of this tendency in them. It's perfectly normal to find ourselves a little edgy or uncomfortable when we encounter someone who is very different from us and the people we live around. In fact, noticing that we feel this way is the best first step toward turning that slightly uncomfortable feeling into welcome rather than hatred.

BUT I THOUGHT I WAS COOL WITH THAT

In 1998, three scientists began a nonprofit organization and research collaboration that studied people's subconscious beliefs and attitudes in order to educate the public about hidden biases and prejudices. They called it Project Implicit, and over the years the program has sponsored a lot of research into the biases we all have. Today, Project Implicit offers the Implicit Attitudes Test (IAT), an online test—actually, a group of tests—that collects data about hidden biases. You can take the IAT yourself at http://implicit.harvard.edu/implicit. The data is useful for research, but it is also very eye-opening for individuals who take the tests. People are often surprised to learn that they have biases that they weren't aware of, and even biases that they are ashamed of. A person who is quick to condemn ageism,

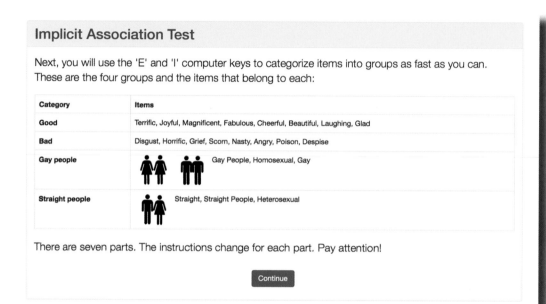

> Project Implicit gives participants a glimpse into prejudices they didn't even know they had.

for example, might be shocked when his or her IAT results show that he or she has a strong preference for young people over old people.

You are not alone in your biases. Studies have shown that everyone has at least some biases and prejudices—sometimes people are even biased against groups to which they themselves belong! You can find women who believe that females are unfit to run large corporations or teenagers who believe all teens are irresponsible. One study found that female scientists evaluated research less favorably when they thought it had been done by a woman than when they thought it was done by a man—even though it was the same research. Having unconscious or implicit biases doesn't make you a bad person; in fact, it is quite normal. It is through discovering and acknowledging those biases that you will grow as a person. Put in the effort to recognize when implicit bias is affecting your own behavior in ways you don't like, so you can change that behavior before any harm is done.

One of the biggest advantages to understanding your own implicit biases is that it helps you understand the biases of others. Even people with some very unhealthy biases may be quite a lot like you—their prejudices are just different and perhaps a lot stronger. This does not mean that discrimination is acceptable—it is absolutely not! But it does benefit you to know your opponents before you begin a conversation with them. And if you are going to speak for change about anything—especially about LGBTQ+ discrimination—it helps to begin with empathy.

MYTHS AND FACTS

MYTH

Antidiscrimination laws give LGBTQ+ citizens special rights.

Fact

LGBTQ+ non-discrimination laws are just like the laws already on the books to protect people from discrimination based on race, religion, and so on. Laws aimed at protecting LGBTQ+ Americans simply add the categories "sexual orientation" and "gender identity" to the list of characteristics already protected by law.

MYTH

LGBTQ+ nondiscrimination laws infringe on the liberties of people whose religion forbids homosexuality.

Fact

Federal law already prohibits discrimination on the basis of religion (which protects religions that oppose homosexuality as well as those that don't). Laws that forbid LGBTQ+ discrimination typically exempt churches. However, courts have ruled repeatedly that nondiscrimination laws that regulate commercial activity, such as those banning hospitals or restaurants from turning people away based on their race, sexual orientation, gender identity, or any other protected characteristic, do not violate the first amendment protection of freedom of speech and religious liberty.

MYTH

With Donald Trump as president, the Supreme Court decision upholding the rights of same-sex couples to marry is likely to be overturned.

Fact

While it is possible that a leader in Donald Trump's position could appoint enough justices to tip the court's balance in an anti-LGBTQ+ direction, it is unlikely that the court would overturn the gay marriage ruling. In order for the court to reverse its historical decision on gay marriage, a plaintiff would have to prove that they had standing to bring a case before the court, and that would require proving that they had been harmed by someone's else's right to get married. Since this would be a very difficult argument to make, same-sex marriage is safe for now.

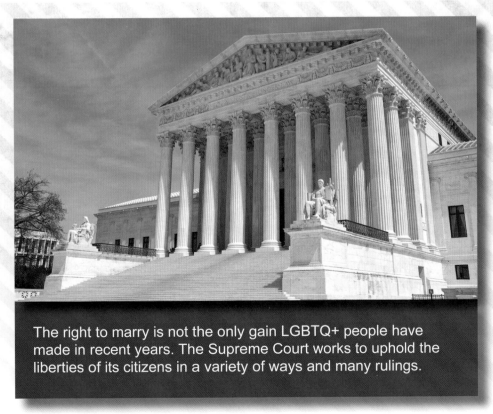

The right to marry is not the only gain LGBTQ+ people have made in recent years. The Supreme Court works to uphold the liberties of its citizens in a variety of ways and many rulings.

CHAPTER THREE

DISCRIMINATION HAPPENS

In addition to marriage equality, LGBTQ+ Americans have seen some other significant gains in recent years. In 2009, President Barack Obama signed into law the first-ever Hate Crimes Act that covers LGBTQ+ Americans. As of December 2010, gays and lesbians have been able to serve openly in the US military, and in July 2016, the US military ended the ban on transgender people serving openly. Boy Scouts of America ended their ban on gay scouts in 2013, and began to allow openly gay scout leaders to participate in 2015. In January 2017, the Boy Scouts began accepting transgender boys into the organization. An article in the *New York Times* said that the change in the Boy Scouts' policy "may help a new generation of Americans think more rationally and compassionately about gender identity." And indeed, it may. However, these gains—especially the Supreme Court's ruling on marriage equality, which had so much positive attention in the media—may give a false sense of progress when it comes to LGBTQ+ rights.

A den leader and gay scout embrace after the announcement that Boy Scouts of America will no longer discriminate against openly gay youth members in 2013. Since then, the organization has also lifted their ban on adults and leaders.

STILL A LONG WAY TO GO

According to a 2016 survey by the LGBTQ+ rights advocacy organization GLAAD, half of non-LGBTQ+ Americans think that "gay people have the same rights as everybody else." But as we have seen, that is not true. LGBTQ+ Americans still face discrimination in almost every facet of life, and sadly, much of the discrimination is perfectly legal. In over half of states,

Under the Obama administration's regulations, the job of Ashley Lang, a transgender TSA worker, was reinstated with back pay after she was illegally fired for using the women's room at the airport where she worked.

landlords can legally evict same-sex couples; in thirty-one states, it is legal to fire an employee because he or she is LGBTQ+. Surveys find that as many as eight out of ten students who are LGBTQ+ (or perceived to be LGBTQ+) experience bullying and other forms of harassment in schools. Thirty-six states have no laws to protect these students, though federal laws do offer some protections for LGBTQ+ students.

In May of 2016, the Obama administration issued guidelines to public schools providing a standard policy on how schools should resolve issues relating to transgender students, making sure transgender students would be allowed to use the restroom that matched their gender identity rather than the gender they were assigned at birth. However, less than a year later, a newly elected President Donald Trump rescinded these protections, leaving it to various states and school districts to either offer the protections themselves or, in the case of most states, not offer them at all.

HOW TO STAND UP FOR YOUR RIGHTS

Knowing your rights is one thing, but insisting that they are honored is quite another. Here are a few tips for making sure your legal rights are respected:

- If you think your rights have been violated, make sure you report the incident.
- Keep a record of the incident, including the date or dates it happened, and as many specifics as you can. If the school asks you to fill out any forms, keep copies for yourself.
- Be calm and respectful at all times. Don't give the school an excuse to give you grief.
- Ask for help and guidance from national organizations such as the American Civil Liberties Union (ACLU).

SOME RIGHTS REMAIN

LGBTQ+ students do have some rights and protections against discrimination. A federal law called Title IX requires public schools to treat incidents of bullying, harassment, name-calling, and physical assaults on LGBTQ+ students in the same way they would address those issues for non-LGBTQ+ students. Schools must also protect the privacy of LGBTQ+ students. Courts have ruled that outing LGBTQ+ kids or threatening to out them is a violation of the constitutionally guaranteed right to privacy. This includes telling an LGBTQ+ student's parents, if the student does not want them informed.

Schools must respect students' right to free speech. LGBTQ+ students cannot be prevented from expressing their gender identity at school. Schools have the right to make rules about what students can and cannot wear to school (requiring uniforms or forbidding shorts or excessively worn jeans, for example), but they cannot legally prevent a male from dressing in traditionally female clothing or vice versa. If a school allows students to wear T-shirts with slogans, that school cannot prevent students from wearing LGBTQ+-themed T-shirts, such as a gay pride shirt (though they can ban obscene images or slogans). Nor can schools prevent LGBTQ+ students from talking about their sexual orientation with other students, though teachers do have the right to control class discussions. The First Amendment to the Constitution and the equal protection clause of the Fourteenth Amendment guarantees the rights of LGBTQ+ students to take a person of their same gender to the prom and other school events.

These rights apply to transgender students as well as gay, lesbian, and bisexual students, but some rights that

A year after becoming his North Carolina high school's first transgender homecoming king, Blake Brockington committed suicide at age eighteen. He had been a strong activist, working to combat transphobia, racism, and police brutality.

would pertain to transgender students are still working their way through the courts and vary from state to state. These include the right to be called by the name and pronoun the student prefers, to be listed on school records by his or her preferred gender, or, as we saw above, to be able to use the locker room or bathroom that matches his or her gender identity rather than the gender he or she was assigned at birth.

Though discrimination against LGBTQ+ Americans is still very much a problem, there are some protections, especially for students. And you can't stand up for your rights and the rights of your fellow students until you know them.

10 GREAT QUESTIONS
TO ASK AN LGBTQ+ RIGHTS ACTIVIST

1. I am gay, but not yet out. I want to stand up for other LGBTQ+ kids who are getting grief at school, but I'm afraid if I do so, it will out me before I'm ready. How can I help from the closet?

2. I have always been very supportive of LGBTQ+ rights, but when one of my best friends told me that she is really a guy, I was totally confused and upset. How can I let him know that I really do care, but I just need some time to get used to the idea?

3. The majority of Americans may support LGBTQ+ equality, but they don't live in my town. What can I do to make a difference in a place where there is so much resistance to LGBTQ+ rights?

4. Plenty of things go on at my school that I suspect are illegal, but pointing this out to the teachers and administration would only get me in trouble. Is there a safe way I can make sure the laws are observed?

5. Speaking up when you see injustice is a great idea, but I am extremely shy. Speaking up about what I want for lunch is difficult. How can shy people make it clear that they object to discrimination?

6. I would like to join an LGBTQ+ rights organization, but there are no groups in my area. Does online activism really work?

7. How do I start a Gay-Straight Alliance at my school?

8. Do you need permits or permission of some kind to have a Pride Parade or an LGBTQ+ demonstration?

9. Some kids at my school think there is no harm in words like fag and homo. How can I convince them that that kind of language really does hurt?

10. I totally support LGBTQ+ rights—but even so, I suspect I have some implicit bias myself. How can I examine and get rid of it?

CHAPTER FOUR

CHANGING YOUR SCHOOL

While it is important to know—and insist upon—the legal rights of LGBTQ+ students, much of the discrimination you will see is not easily addressed by pointing out the legal rights of the LGBTQ+ community. Often, the best approach is not through court but in the classroom or the lunchroom. A great amount can be done to end discrimination by addressing the problem before the discrimination actually happens. Education and awareness are powerful tools in the battle to end LGBTQ+ discrimination.

TO KNOW ME IS TO LOVE ME

Many people were surprised at how quickly attitudes toward homosexuality changed in the United States—more than a 45 percent jump in approval in just over two decades, a virtually unprecedented change in public opinion in such a short period of time. Various theories have been offered to explain the shift. Some of it is simply due to a generational shift. People under thirty are almost entirely supportive of LGBTQ+ rights.

If this seems wildly optimistic to you, keep in mind that even if only 15 percent of the under-thirty population is hostile to LGBTQ+ people, depending on where you live you may have met a disproportionate number of them. According to a survey released in 2014 by Public Religion Research Institute (PRRI), a non-partisan research organization, only 44 percent of rural Americans favored same-sex marriage—and that number is considerably lower among older rural Americans. However, generational change is slow and cannot begin to account for the pace of the shift in attitudes.

Another factor is the increasingly positive image of LGBTQ+ people in films and on television. Probably the most significant factor is simply visibility, or exposure to LGBTQ+ individuals. The more LGBTQ+ people come out, the more the rest of the culture comes to accept them. In the early 1990s, polls showed that only about 20–30 percent of Americans knew someone who was LGBTQ+. By the turn of the century, that figure had reached 50 percent, and now that number is close to 90 percent. Getting to know LGBTQ+ classmates, neighbors, and family members has normalized being LGBTQ+.

LET'S ALL COME OUT TOGETHER

There are many things students—LGBTQ+ or not—can do to help fellow students (and teachers) get to know LGBTQ+ people, even in schools where few or no students are out. Students can do book reports on LGBTQ+ literary and historical figures; you may be surprised to learn how many options you have. School assemblies and class projects often offer opportunities

When well-loved comedian Ellen DeGeneres came out as lesbian, she helped change the nation's attitudes toward LGBTQ+ people.

to speak about LGBTQ+ issues. Asking an LGBTQ+ relative or member of the community to speak at career day or similar events or requesting LGBTQ+ writers to do author visits can be great ways to help schools get to know LGBTQ+ people. Gay-Straight Alliance clubs are extracurricular groups designed to be a safe place for LGBTQ+ and straight high school and college students to talk about sexual orientation and gender identity. Schools that start GSAs are taking a huge step toward equal education on LGBTQ+ issues.

SAFE SPACE

Until **LGBTQ+ discrimination is completely eliminated, many LGBTQ+ students will often feel uncomfortable and sometimes unsafe at school. When teachers create designated safe spaces at schools, the school experience is much, much better for LGBTQ+ kids. Research has shown that they not only feel safer, they also skip class less often and achieve higher grades. Having an official safe space can also send a powerful message to the rest of the student body and administration about how much LGBTQ+ students need protections. GLSEN (pronounced "glisten")—a national organization working to make sure all students, no matter what their sexual orientation, gender identity, or gender expression, are respected and**

Student Ambassadors share the stage with cochairs Jim Spielding and Jim Parsons (*center*) at the 2016 GLSEN Respect Awards ceremony.

kept safe in school—provides a safe space kit, which you can access online at http://glsen.org. It gives teachers and schools help setting up a safe space: a welcoming, warm, supportive environment for LGBTQ+ students. LGBTQ+ students and their allies can share the kit with sympathetic teachers and offer to help them get the program going.

It is not always physically or emotionally safe for LGBTQ+ people to come out, and the decision about if and when to come out is very personal. No one should ever be pushed to make that decision before they are ready. However, those who are already out, as well as friends and allies of LGBTQ+ students, can make a big difference in changing attitudes and thus ending the fear of discrimination.

TEXTBOOK QUEERS

Students are often surprised to learn that many of the people they study in history and literature classes were LGBTQ+. Some were openly so, or at least open enough that historians are sure of their sexual orientation. Others left enough clues to make a good case. The astronaut Sally Ride was a lesbian, writer Virginia Woolf and blues singer Billie Holiday were bisexual, poet Langston Hughes and playwright Tennessee Williams were gay. Poet Walt Whitman, although he never publicly admitted it, is widely believed to have been gay (or perhaps pansexual). Some scholars think that Emily Dickinson may have been a lesbian. And some evidence from first lady Eleanor Roosevelt's correspondence with her long-time friend and openly lesbian companion, Lorena Hickok, suggests the two may have had a romantic relationship (though many

Irish playwright Oscar Wilde is one of many LGBTQ+ people you'll study in school. Unfortunately, he was born in 1854 and lived in a time when being gay was not accepted; he was imprisoned for his sexuality.

people dispute this, and there is also evidence in the letters that Mrs. Roosevelt was not Hickok's lover). Whether she was LGBTQ+ or not, Eleanor Roosevelt was one of the strongest pre-Stonewall supporters of LGBTQ+ rights. Introducing your school to more LGBTQ+ people may just take cracking the books.

WHEN YOU SEE IT, STOP IT

Even though acceptance of homosexuality has rapidly increased in recent decades, and acceptance of transgender and other gender nonconforming people is on the rise as well, depending on where you live, you still may see or experience a lot of discrimination. History has shown that one of the best ways to end discrimination of any kind is to refuse to ignore it. When people look the other way and hope that things will get better, they usually just get worse. It is when people speak up when they see discrimination and refuse to accept it that things start to change.

Speaking up doesn't mean being confrontational—simply saying, "I don't appreciate being spoken to like that," or "Hey, don't talk to my friend that way," can defuse a lot of situations. It is also important to report any violations of legal rights. Schools and administrators can't protect anyone's rights if they don't know they are being violated. Of course, it is essential to always report any outright acts of bullying or threats of violence to the authorities. Safety is paramount, and if things look like they are about to get out of hand, leaving the scene is almost always the best idea. If another person is being harmed or threatened, it is essential to get help immediately.

It is important to remember that confronting LGBTQ+ discrimination is not just the responsibility of the victim. The more people who stand up and speak up, the easier it will be to stop it. Preventing LGBTQ+ discrimination or stopping it in its tracks is always a team effort. LGBTQ+ students, their families, friends, classmates, and teachers all have a responsibility to stop it when they see it.

CHAPTER FIVE

CHANGING THE WORLD

School may be where young people are most likely to encounter LGBTQ+ discrimination, but much more discrimination is happening out there in the larger world. As we have seen, among Americans over thirty years old, there is far less support for LGBTQ+ rights than among younger people. Despite recent gains, discrimination in housing, employment, health care, and other areas is still a huge problem for LGBTQ+ people. Kids and teens often think that because they are still students and not yet old enough to vote there is not much they can do to address discrimination in the world outside of their own school community. But young people are citizens, too, and there is actually a tremendous amount they can do—even before they are old enough to make their feelings known in the ballot box.

SPEAKING TRUTH TO POWER

Members of Congress, state houses, and city councils represent everyone in their districts, not just voters. Obviously, they listen most closely to the people who have the power to vote them out of office, but that doesn't mean young people can't influence

A long-time supporter of gay rights, Massachusetts Governor A. Paul Cellucci renewed the executive office's commitment to combat suicide and violence affecting gay and lesbian youth.

their decisions. Educating the public and advocating for LGBTQ+ rights can influence voters, who in turn influence elected officials. Talking with friends, family, and neighbors and sharing information about LGBTQ+ issues and pending legislation on social media and other platforms, is a great way to get the word out to voters. When young people are well-informed, accurate, and persuasive, yet nonconfrontational, in addressing these issues, they can be a powerful force for change in the rest of society.

Sometimes, young people can have a very powerful and direct effect on elected officials. In 1993, when the Massachusetts state legislature was considering legislation to prohibit discrimination in public schools on the basis of sexual orientation, thousands of students, both LGBTQ+ and straight, wrote letters, spoke at rallies, and met with their state representatives to share their experiences of bullying and harassment and show their leaders the faces of the students this legislation would protect. Massachusetts' Gay and Lesbian Student Rights Law—the first state law of its kind anywhere in the United States—was passed because young people got involved with the political process.

WORKING ON THE INSIDE

Another way young people can get involved in the political process before they are old enough to vote is by supporting LGBTQ+ political candidates, both local and national, or candidates who are committed supporters of LGBTQ+ rights. This can mean discussing the candidate with friends and relatives, posting information and campaign advertisements on social media, or simply sporting the candidate's T-shirt or bumper sticker.

GET OUT THE VOTE

Though there is a lot you can do even before you're old enough to vote, it is important to know when and how to get registered once you are old enough; in some states, you don't even have to wait until you're eighteen. That's right—a few states allow seventeen-year-olds to vote in primary elections if they will be eighteen in time for the general election. Voter registration is handled at the

Even before you are old enough to vote, there is a lot you can do to influence policy and help elect candidates who support LGBTQ+ issues.

county level, so you'll need to call your county courthouse to find out how and when to register and where to go to vote on the big day. The rules and deadlines for registering vary from state to state, and sometimes even from year to year. If you are getting close to voting age, call your local office and find out what you need to do to be registered in time to vote as soon as you're old enough. And don't wait for the next presidential election! Local elections are important, too. In fact, if you want to get involved with politics, your local government is the best place to start.

If you aren't old enough to vote and won't be anytime soon, you can still help out by making sure older friends and siblings understand what is at stake and how to get registered. One of the best things you can do as a nonvoter is to help ensure that those who can vote, do vote.

Young people who really want to get involved can go even further; political candidates need all the help they can get. By volunteering to pass out flyers, work phone banks, speak at neighborhood meetings, and do any of the myriad other tasks involved in running for office, young people can have far more power in determining who makes the decisions that affect their lives—and all lives—than some people have by simply voting every few years. By the time these politically active youths finally turn eighteen and become eligible to vote, they've already been responsible for a lot of change.

IS HATE A CRIME?

Verbal expressions of hatred and abuse are among the most visible and disturbing examples of discrimination. It's very tempting for schools and other institutions to pass rules or laws forbidding such language. On the surface, it sounds like a great idea: hate speech is bad, so ban it. However, the same first amendment right to free speech that guarantees the rights of LGBTQ+ Americans

This hat is a direct reaction to President Donald Trump's 2016 campaign slogan "Make America Great Again." Responding to hate speech and contradictory viewpoints with love speech is often the most effective approach.

to express their gender identities (and to say whatever else they want to) also guarantees that other people can say what they like about that—even if it is hate-filled and offensive.

And oddly enough, there can be an advantage of sorts—beyond a commitment to free speech for everyone—to letting haters have their say. When hate is expressed openly, everyone can see it for what it is and counter it with their own free speech.

Hate crimes are another matter. The FBI defines a hate crime as a "criminal offense against a person or property motivated in whole or in part by an offender's bias against a race, religion, disability, sexual orientation, ethnicity, gender, or gender identity." Though the FBI points out that hate itself is not a crime and the Bureau is very mindful of First Amendment rights, they do take hate crimes very seriously because, as they state on the FBI website, "Hate crimes are the highest priority of the FBI's Civil Rights program, not only because of the devastating impact they have on families and communities, but also because groups that preach hatred and intolerance can plant the seed of terrorism here in our country."

Young people who get involved with campaigns often discover they have a taste for politics and might one day like to run for office themselves. There are many organizations who work with young people to train them to run for political office, whether at the local, state, or national level. Volunteering with LGBTQ+ advocacy groups such as the Human Rights Campaign or GLSEN can be a great way not only to learn more about LGBTQ+ issues and how to confront discrimination, but also can be excellent experience for running for office in the years to come.

Getting involved in school politics by running for student government or a leadership position in an extracurricular organization can also be an enriching experience. Who knows, that student who once organized the first Gay-Straight Alliance club at your school might one day become your state senator—and that student could be you. Even students who never plan to run for office will find that there are many ways to engage in the political process in their own communities to help end LGBTQ+ discrimination and ensure all Americans enjoy the rights and freedoms that are fundamental to our nation.

CHAPTER SIX

THE FUTURE

There is no doubt that these are challenging times for the LGBTQ+ community. Many states offer no protection for LGBTQ+ rights, and federal protections are often ignored. Other protections, such as federal guidelines for transgender students, are being rolled back. But this is no time to lose heart. More than ever before, people are aware of the needs and challenges facing LGBTQ+ Americans, and increasing numbers of straight Americans have the will and the courage to stand up to LGBTQ+ discrimination. Americans, young and old, LGBTQ+-identifying or not, are signing petitions, joining marches, and calling their legislators to demand an end to LGBTQ+ discrimination. Corporations have pulled money out of states that pass religious-freedom laws to legalize LGBTQ+ discrimination. Citizens of all sexual orientations and gender identities are increasingly likely to speak up when they witness acts of LGBTQ+ discrimination.

IN THE HALLS OF POWER

While as of 2017, there are only six openly LGBTQ+ members in the United States House of Representatives

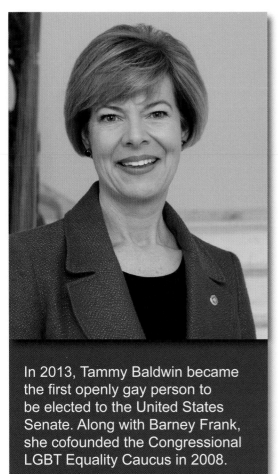

In 2013, Tammy Baldwin became the first openly gay person to be elected to the United States Senate. Along with Barney Frank, she cofounded the Congressional LGBT Equality Caucus in 2008.

and one openly LGBTQ+ member in the US Senate (Tammy Baldwin, Wisconsin), there are many more LGBTQ+ candidates running for and winning state and local offices, which is a good sign for the future. And it doesn't take parity (when the proportion of LGBTQ+ to straight representatives matches that of the population) to make a difference.

According to the Gay and Lesbian Victory Institute, an organization that works to get more LGBTQ+ candidates elected to public office, a small number of LGBTQ+ representatives in a state legislature can still influence their colleagues to pass laws that prevent LGBTQ+ discrimination. Studies have shown that the more openly LGBTQ+ public officials there are at any level or position in a given state, the more equality there is in that state. According to a 2016 report by the Victory Institute, "Nearly 70 percent of the states with high levels of LGBTQ+ equality have three or more openly LGBTQ+ people serving in their state legislatures."

SOMEBODY HAS TO GO FIRST

Although as of 2017 there were only seven LGBTQ+ members of the United States Congress, the LGBTQ+ community has been more widely represented in the halls of power than that number suggests—and somebody had to be the first.

- Elaine Noble of Massachusetts was the first openly lesbian or gay candidate elected to a state legislature.
- Cathy Woolard of Atlanta, Georgia, was the first openly gay president of a city council.
- Jim McGreevey of New Jersey was the first openly gay governor in the United States.
- Kate Brown of Oregon was the first openly bisexual governor and the first LGBTQ+ governor to be out when taking office.
- Maura Healey of Massachusetts was the first openly lesbian state attorney general.

Since these politicians were brave enough to come out, more and more LGBTQ+ Americans have been willing to step up and serve their country in political office.

The Student Non-Discrimination Act, which would prohibit public schools from discriminating against students based on actual or perceived sexual orientation or gender identity, was introduced into the United States Congress in 2015. It did not pass, but it did garner the support of every Democratic senator and seven Republicans. The sponsors of the bill intend to keep trying to push through this and other legislation to protect LGBTQ+ rights, such as bills to prevent LGBTQ+ discrimination in housing, employment, and health care.

SEEING THROUGH THE SMOKE AND MIRRORS

Though some states are passing discriminatory laws aimed at the LGBTQ+ community, there are good signs on the local level. In the 2016 elections, the only incumbent governor to lose his or her reelection bid was Pat McCrory, the anti-LGBTQ+ governor of North Carolina who supported House Bill 2 (also known as the bathroom bill). This infamous legislation would have, among other anti-LGBTQ+ provisions, required people to use public restrooms and changing facilities that accord with the gender they were assigned at birth, rather than the gender with which they identify. HB2 was the critical issue that cost McCrory the election. Even voters who supported Donald Trump in that election voted overwhelmingly against the anti-LGBTQ+ Republican governor. Clearly, despite recent setbacks for progressives, Americans are not reversing all of their opinions on LGBTQ+ rights.

One of the reasons for the backlash against North Carolina's HB2 was that when LGBTQ+ people—and

As more LGBTQ+ Americans and their supporters speak out, attitudes and laws will change for the better. Here, a group of young people protest North Carolina's House Bill 2 law restricting transgender rights.

particularly transgender people—spoke out about it, the rest of the community at large got a chance to hear their stories and attach names and faces to the people and families who are harmed by these discriminatory laws. For most people, it is much easier to discriminate against seemingly faceless groups than against known individuals. When the ridiculous fictions of gay men "recruiting" school children or transgender women stalking other women in restrooms are countered by the stories and faces of very real, very human Americans who just want to live their lives with equal access to the same rights and freedoms as everyone else, support for LGBTQ+ discrimination withers very quickly.

IT'S JUST GOOD BUSINESS

One of the reasons recent anti-LGBTQ+ legislation has been met with such resistance is because LGBTQ+ discrimination is bad for business—and some of the biggest supporters of LGBTQ+ equality are big businesses. Google has been widely lauded for its support of LGBTQ+ equality, but other companies have made their support clear as well. When a Starbucks investor criticized the company's CEO, Howard Schultz, by speculating that the company's outspoken support for LGBTQ+ issues could hurt the company's bottom line, Schultz reminded the investor that if he was so concerned, he could sell his Starbucks stock and invest elsewhere.

Chevron may not be a company you associate with progressive values, but the giant energy company offers benefits to same-sex couples and transgender employees and includes nondiscrimination in its company policies. Other

A pride flag flutters in Seattle, Washington, on top of the headquarters of Starbucks, one of many US companies that have actively and visibly shown their support for LGBTQ+ rights.

companies that are known for supporting LGBTQ+ rights are Apple (whose CEO is openly gay), Doritos (a company that once released special rainbow edition packaging in support of a program to reduce suicides of LGBTQ+ teens), Levi's, Oreo's, Home Depot, Nike, Target, Adidas, Gap, Coca-Cola, and many other companies both large and small.

As more Americans step up and tell their individual stories, a broader listenership will begin to see these restrictions to LGBTQ+ rights for what they are: smoke and mirrors working to steal attention from other, equally dangerous issues facing LGBTQ+ people and their fundamental, inalienable rights. There are still companies that do not want to employ, landlords who do not want to rent to, and insurance companies that do not want to extend health care benefits to LGBTQ+ Americans.

However, the election of seven LGBTQ+ members of Congress, the repeal of a bathroom bill here, and a passage of an anti-LGBTQ+ bullying bill there are not minor victories in an overall dismal landscape, even though it may seem that way at times. They are strong indications that the United States is taking two steps forward for each step backward in the march toward full equality for everyone and the end to LGBTQ+ discrimination. And there is reason to expect that pace to increase, as young people—who overwhelmingly support LGBTQ+ rights—grow older and move into more positions of power and authority. The world will only get better for LGBTQ+ people and everyone else.

GLOSSARY

allies People who do not identify as LGBTQ+ themselves, but support LGBTQ+ rights.

asexual Lacking any sexual attraction or desire toward others.

binary A system that has two as its base; in the case of gender, this would be male and female.

cisgender A person whose gender identity corresponds with the gender they were assigned at birth.

disproportionate Larger or smaller than would be expected in relation to something else.

district An area of a city, state, or nation organized for administrative purpose, such as a US Congressional district.

extracurricular An activity or project completed outside the normal course of study.

gender The state of being male, female, or neither based on social rather than biological differences.

gender identity A person's perception of having a particular gender.

heterosexual Sexually attracted to people of the opposite gender.

implicit Implied but not stated; woven into the fabric of something.

inclusive Involving or embracing any section of society; opposite of exclusive.

intersex A term used for a variety of conditions in which a person is born with a variation in their sex characteristics, inclusive of chromosomes, gonads, sex hormones, or genitals, that does not fit within the standard medical definitions for male or female bodies.

microaggression A subtle but offensive comment or action directed at a minority group that is often unintentional but reinforces a stereotype.

nonconforming Going against rules, standards, or laws.

nonpartisan Not adhering to the values or goals of any particular political party or philosophical position.

pansexual Being sexually attracted to any sex, gender, or gender identity.

parity The state of being equal or equivalent.

plaintiff The individual or other entity that brings a lawsuit against another party.

progressives People or political groups who support social reform.

rescind To take back, invalidate, or repeal, as in an agreement or law.

sexual orientation A person's sexual identity in relation to the gender to which they are attracted; being heterosexual, homosexual, or bisexual.

standing In the legal sense, having sufficient proof of harm to able to bring a lawsuit in a particular circumstance.

subconscious Feelings or behaviors that are below the awareness of the person exhibiting them.

visibility Being able to see or be seen.

FOR MORE INFORMATION

American Civil Liberties Union
125 Broad Street, 18th Floor
New York, NY 10001
(212) 549-2500
Website: https://www.aclu.org
An organization that works to defend and protect the
individual rights and liberties that are guaranteed by
the Constitution of the United States.

Egale Canada Human Rights Trust
185 Carlton Street
Toronto, ON M5A 2K7
Canada
(888) 204-7777
Website: http://egale.ca/about/
A Canadian Nation Charity that works to support LGBT
human rights.

Gay Lesbian and Straight Education Network (GLSEN)
110 William Street, 30th Floor
New York, NY 10038
(212) 727-0135
Email: Info@glsen.org
Website: http://www.glsen.org
An organization dedicated to making sure that every
student in every school, no matter what sexual
orientation, gender identity, or gender expression, is
valued and respected.

GSA Network
1611 Telegraph Avenue, Suite 1002
Oakland, CA 94612
(415) 552-4229

Email: Info@gsanetwork.org
Website: http://gsanetwork.org
A national network of gay-straight alliance groups that
  empowers and trains LGBTQ+ youth to create safer
  schools and healthier communities.

LGBT Youthline
Wood Street Post Office
PO Box 73118
Toronto, ON M4Y 2W5
Canada
(800) 268-9688
Website: http://www.youthline.ca
A Canadian organization that provides LGBTQ+ peer-to-
  peer support.

Teaching Tolerance
400 Washington Avenue
Montgomery, AL 36104
(888) 414-7752
Website: https://www.splcenter.org/teaching-tolerance
A project of the Southern Poverty Law Center, a group
  dedicated to combatting prejudice among youth and
  promoting equality, inclusiveness, and equitable
  learning environments in the classroom.

WEBSITES

Because of the changing nature of internet links, Rosen
Publishing has developed an online list of websites
related to the subject of this book. This site is updated
regularly. Please use this link to access this list:

http://www.rosenlinks.com/SPKUP/LGBTQ+

FOR FURTHER READING

Albertalli, Becky. *Simon and the Homo Sapiens Agenda*. New York, NY: HarperCollins, 2015.

Bronski, Michael. *A Queer History of the United States*. Boston, MA: Beacon Press, 2011.

Garden, Nancy. *Hear Us Out: Lesbian and Gay Stories of Struggle, Progress, and Hope, 1950 to the Present*. New York, NY: Farrar, Straus and Giroux, 2007.

Gay, Kathlyn. *Activism: The Ulimate Teen Guide*. Lanham, MD: Rowman & Littlefield, 2016.

Konigsberg, Bill. *Openly Straight*. New York, NY: Scholastic, 2013.

Kuhn, Betsy. *Gay Power! The Stonewall Riots and the Gay Rights Movement, 1969*. Minneapolis, MN: Twenty-First Century Books, 2011.

Kuklin, Susan. *Beyond Magenta: Transgender Teens Speak Out*. Somerville, MA: Candlewick Press, 2014.

Pohlen, Jerome. *Gay & Lesbian History for Kids: The Century-Long Struggle for LGBT Rights*. Chicago, IL: Chicago Review Press, 2016.

Sadowski, Michael. *Safe Is Not Enough: Better Schools for LGBTQ Students*. Cambridge, MA: Harvard Education Press, 2016.

Savage, Dan, and Terry Miller. *It Gets Better: Coming Out, Overcoming Bullying, and Creating a Life Worth Living*. New York, NY: Plume, 2012.

Signorile, Michelangelo. *It's Not Over: Getting Beyond Tolerance, Defeating Homophobia, and Winning True Equality*. New York, NY: Houghton Mifflin Harcourt, 2015.

Thompson, Laurie Ann. *Be a Changemaker: How to Start Something That Matters*. New York, NY: Simon Pulse, 2014.

BIBLIOGRAPHY

Baksh, Kurina. "Workplace Discrimination: The LGBT Workforce." *Huffington Post*, June 22, 2016. http://www.huffingtonpost.com/kurina-baksh/workplace-discrimination-_b_10606030.html.

"Civil Rights 101: Gays and Lesbians." The Leadership Conference. Retrieved February, 2017. http://www.civilrights.org/resources/civilrights101/sexualorientation.html.

Eckholm, Erik. "Next Fight for Gay Rights: Bias in Jobs and Housing." *New York Times*, June 27, 2015. https://www.nytimes.com/2015/06/28/us/gay-rights-leaders-push-for-federal-civil-rights-protections.html?_r=2&mtrref=undefined&assetType=nyt_now.

Green, Emma. "The Federal Government's Reversal: Let the States Deal with Transgender Kids." *The Atlantic*, February 22, 2017. https://www.theatlantic.com/politics/archive/2017/02/transgender-guidance/517530.

Grewal, Daisy. "The Evolution of Prejudice." *Scientific American*, April 5, 2011. https://www.scientificamerican.com/article/evolution-of-prejudice.

Horsley, Scott. "White House Sends Schools Guidance on Transgender Access to Bathrooms." NPR.org, May 13, 2016. http://www.npr.org/sections/thetwo-way/2016/05/13/477896804/obama-administration-to-offer-schools-guidance-on-transgender-bathrooms.

Isidore, Chris. "How Businesses Can Still Discriminate Against LGBTQ People." *CNN Money*, June 26, 2015. http://money.cnn.com/2015/06/26/news/companies/lgbt-discrimination.

Joslin, Courtney. "Protection for Lesbian, Gay, Bisexual, and Transgender Employees Under Title VII of the 1964 Civil Rights Act." *Human Rights Magazine*, vol. 31, no. 3. http://www.americanbar.org/publications /human_rights_magazine_home/human_rights _vol31_2004/summer2004/irr_hr_summer04 _protectlgbt.html.

Kuo, Maggie. "Consciously Combatting Unconscious Bias." *Science*, January 30, 2017. http://www .sciencemag.org/careers/2017/01/consciously -combating-unconscious-bias.

Masci, David. "Key Findings about Americans' Views on Religious Liberty and Nondiscrimination." Pew Research Center, September 28, 2016. http://www. pewresearch.org/fact-tank/2016/09/28/key -findings-about-americans-views-on-religious-liberty -and-nondiscrimination.

McGill, Andres. "Americans Are Embracing Transgender Rights." *The Atlantic*. August 25, 2016. http://www. theatlantic.com/politics/archive/2016/08 /americans-are-embracing-transgender- rights/497444.

Morris, Bonnie J. "History of Lesbian, Gay, and Bisexual Social Movements." American Psychological Association. Retrieved February 2017. http://www .apa.org/pi/lgbt/resources/history.aspx.

Richards, David A. J. *The Case for Gay Rights: From Bowers to Lawrence and Beyond*. Lawrence, KS: University Press of Kansas, 2005.

"Shelby County v. Holder, Attorney General, et al." SupremeCourt.gov. Retrieved February 2017. https://www.supremecourt.gov/opinions/12pdf/12 -96_6k47.pdf.

Signorile, Michelangelo. *It's Not Over: Getting Beyond Tolerance, Defeating Homophobia, and Winning True Equality*. New York, NY: Houghton Mifflin Harcourt, 2015.

"So Far So Fast: Marriage Equality in America." *The Economist,* October 9, 2014. http://www.economist.com/news/briefing/21623671-week-americas-supreme-court-dealt-supporters-gay-marriage-great-victory-we-look.

"Stonewall Riots: The Beginning of the LGBT Movement." The Leadership Conference, June 22, 2009. http://www.civilrights.org/archives/2009/06/449-stonewall.html.

Thoreson, Ryan. "Like Walking Through a Hailstorm: Discrimination Against LGBT Youth in Schools." Human Rights Watch, December 7, 2016. https://www.hrw.org/report/2016/12/07/walking-through-hailstorm/discrimination-against-lgbt-youth-us-schools.

"What Is Discrimination?" Findlaw.org. Retrieved February 2017. http://civilrights.findlaw.com/civil-rights-overview/what-is-discrimination.html.

Zezima, Katie. "Boy Scouts of America Will Allow Transgender Children to Join." *Washington Post*, January 30, 2017. https://www.washingtonpost.com/news/post-nation/wp/2017/01/30/boy-scouts-of-america-will-allow-transgender-children-to-join/?utm_term=.c92423190cdc.

INDEX

B

Boy Scouts of America, 24
bullying, 11, 26–29, 41
businesses, 47, 52–53

C

campaigning for change, 43,
45–46

D

discrimination
discernment versus rejection, 8
forms of in different states, 5
subtle, 11
tribal psychology and overcoming of, 19
unknown versus known
threats, 51

E

economy and LGBTQ+ laws, 47,
52–53
education, discrimination in, 9,
11

F

Federal Bureau of Investigation
and hate crimes, 45
First Amendment rights
free speech rights, 28, 44–45
Title IX protections, 28–29
versus nondiscrimination
laws, 22
Fourteenth Amendment, 28

G

Gay and Lesbian Victory
Institute, 48
gay rights movement, 13
Gay-Straight Alliance (GSA)
clubs, 34, 46
GLAAD, 25
GLSEN, 34–35

H

Hate Crimes Act, 24, 45
HB2 ("bathroom bill"), 15,
50–51
historical LGBTQ+ figures, 36–37
housing discrimination, 9, 15,
25–26

L

legislation, anti-LGBTQ+, 52–53
legislators, openly LGBTQ+, 49s
LGBTQ+, meaning of the acronym, 10

M

Massachusetts' Gay and Lesbian
Students Rights Law, 41

N

nondiscrimination laws, 22
North Carolina and "bathroom
bill," 50

O

Obama, Barack, 24
"outing" of LGBTQ+ students,
28, 36

P

politics
candidates, 41, 43
LGBTQ+ politicians, 48–49
running for office, 43, 46, 49
state government and LGBTQ+
legislators, 48
Public Religion Research
Institute (PRRI), 32
public spaces and bathrooms,
15, 27–28

R

religious-freedom laws, 22, 47
rights
free speech, 44–45
knowing your own, 27
nondiscrimination laws, 22
Title IX, 28–29
Roberts, John, 11–12
Roosevelt, Eleanor, 38–39

S

same-sex marriage
benefits offered by companies,
52
biases against, 26
Supreme Court decision, 4–5,
15, 23
survey of attitudes toward, 32
schools
activities to educate and unify,
32, 34
antidiscrimination policies, 7,
26–27
bullying and hate speech,
26–27
educating through activities, 32,
34
political process to gain
protections, 26, 41, 50
safe space for LGBTQ+
students, 34–35
sexual orientation issues, 4–5,
10, 22, 28, 34, 36–37
Stonewall riots, 12–14
Student Non-Discrimination Act,
50
suicide, 53
Supreme Court and same-sex
marriage ruling, 4–5, 15, 23

T

Title IX, 28–29
tribal psychology, 19
Trump, Donald, 23, 27, 50

U

US Congress, 47–48, 50
US military, 24

V

violence against LGBTQ+ people, 15, 38
voters
educating about LGBTQ+
issues, 41, 43, 50
registration, 42–43
Voting Rights Act, 11–12

W

workplace, discrimination in,
4–5, 9, 14, 15, 26

ABOUT THE AUTHOR

Avery Elizabeth Hurt is a children's writer and journalist who for many years has covered LGBTQ+ issues for several publications, including the *New Physician* magazine. She is thrilled about the recent progress in LGBTQ+ rights and is committed to continuing to work toward full equality for everyone, regardless of sexual orientation or gender identity.

PHOTO CREDITS